Investing Money

A FUN GUIDE

For Kids Ages 8-12 to

Financial Independence

Simi Subhramanian

Copyright © 2023 by Simi Subhramanian

For permissions requests, write to the publisher at the address below:
Publisher: Simi Subhramanian, India
Email: Shaurisimi@gmail.com
Cover design by Simi Subhramanian

Disclaimer: The information provided in this book is for general informational purposes only. The content is based on the topic of investing money and aims to introduce financial concepts to kids ages 8-12 in a fun and educational manner.

Investing involves risks, and individual results may vary. The author and publisher disclaim any liability for any loss or damage incurred by the reader or any third party directly or indirectly as a result of the use or application of the information presented in this book. The content provided in this book should not be misconstrued as financial advice or a recommendation to invest.

The concepts presented in this book are simplified to cater to a young audience and should not replace formal financial education or guidance. Parents, guardians, and educators are encouraged to supplement this book's information with appropriate financial resources and seek the advice of financial professionals when making investment decisions.

It is essential to foster responsible financial habits and instil the value of financial independence and literacy from an early age. This book serves as a starting point to encourage young readers' interest in financial concepts, and further exploration is encouraged to enhance their understanding of personal finance and investment options.

Author Profile

Simi Subhramanian is an accomplished author and dedicated educator with a passion for teaching. She holds a range of qualifications in the teaching profession, including certifications from the Asian College of Teachers, TQUK (Training Qualifications UK), and Montessori Europe. With an extensive educational background, Simi brings a wealth of knowledge and expertise to her writing.

Simi's journey in education began at the Asian College of Teachers in Mumbai, India. There, she honed her teaching skills and gained a deep understanding of pedagogical principles. Armed with this foundation, she embarked on a mission to inspire and educate students of all ages through her writing.

Further enriching her qualifications, Simi pursued additional certifications from TQUK and Montessori Europe. These certifications expanded her repertoire of teaching methodologies and deepened her understanding of diverse learning styles. With these enhanced skills, she has been able to create engaging and effective educational content that caters to a wide range of learners.

Simi's writing reflects her commitment to excellence in education. She understands that effective teaching goes beyond imparting knowledge; it requires creativity, empathy, and the ability to connect with students on a deeper level. Her dedication to fostering a love of learning and promoting critical thinking is evident in her work.

Through her writing, Simi aims to inspire and empower students, encouraging them to reach their full potential. Her books and educational materials cover a wide range of subjects, from language arts to science and mathematics. Simi's approach emphasizes active learning, interactivity, and real-world applications to ensure students grasp concepts thoroughly.

With her diverse qualifications and years of experience in the teaching profession, Simi Subhramanian has established herself as a trusted and respected author in the education field. Her passion for teaching shines through in her writing, making her work both informative and engaging.

Simi continues to stay abreast of the latest developments in education and actively seeks innovative teaching approaches. By incorporating emerging trends and methodologies into her writing, she ensures that her educational materials remain relevant and effective.

Simi Subhramanian's author profile represents a seamless integration of her teaching qualifications from the Asian College of Teachers, TQUK, and Montessori Europe. Her expertise and dedication make her a valuable asset in the realm of educational literature, as she strives to make a positive impact on students' lives through her insightful and engaging content.

Introduction

Welcome, young adventurers, to a world of endless possibilities! Have you ever wondered what makes money so special and how it can help you achieve incredible things? If you're curious about the secrets of turning your pocket change into a magical force that brings dreams to life, then this book is your ultimate guide!

Prepare to unlock the door to a thrilling realm where saving, investing, and financial independence unite in a symphony of excitement. Yes, you heard it right - money can be exciting! Forget about the idea that money is only for grown-ups in suits; it's time to discover how kids like you can wield the power of investing to shape your future.

In this enchanting journey, we'll embark on thrilling adventures and unravel the mysteries of the financial universe. From the glittering coins that jingle in your piggy bank to the dazzling world of stocks and bonds, you'll explore it all with awe and wonder. Picture yourself as a young magician, learning the spells that transform your hard-earned money into a prosperous and fulfilling life.

Imagine this: you set a goal to buy your favourite toy, but instead of just wishing for it, you unleash the force of investing. As you watch your money grow like a mystical garden, you'll be amazed at how it multiplies over time, becoming more powerful with each passing day. And when the time is right, you'll open your treasure chest of savings and find that it has grown into something even more magnificent than you ever imagined!

But beware, young readers, for every journey has its challenges. Along the way, you'll encounter mysterious creatures called "risks" that might try to block your path. But fear not, for this book is equipped with powerful tools to help you navigate through the twists and turns of the investing world. You'll learn how to befriend these creatures, tame them, and turn them into allies, ensuring your success on this captivating quest.

As we delve deeper into the realm of investing, you'll be introduced to inspiring stories of other young adventurers who have conquered financial mountains, showing you that you too have the courage to reach great heights. Moreover, you'll discover the art of giving, where your investments can make a difference in the lives of others, creating a ripple of kindness and positive change in the world.

So, my dear readers, fasten your seatbelts, for this journey is not just about

acquiring riches - it's about discovering the true magic within you. By the time you turn the final page, you'll be equipped with the wisdom and knowledge to steer your financial destiny. You'll possess the key to financial independence, the secret of making money work for you, and the ability to turn your dreams into reality.

Are you ready to embark on this thrilling adventure of Investing Money: A Fun Guide for Kids Ages 8-12 to Financial Independence? Then let's set sail on a magical voyage where dreams take flight, and the power of investing awaits your grasp!

Chapter 1
What is Money?

What is?

Imagine a world without money, where we had to barter or trade goods for everything we wanted. Picture this: you have a shiny new toy, but you really want some delicious cookies. Without money, you would need to find someone who loves toys as much as you love cookies and is willing to exchange their cookies for your toy. It sounds complicated, doesn't it? Luckily, we don't have to live in a world like that because we have something incredible called "money." Money is like a magical bridge that connects our desires and dreams with the things we want. It's a special tool that allows us to exchange goods and services with ease. From the moment we start understanding the world around us, money plays a significant role in our lives.

The Origins of Money

Long, long ago, in ancient times, people realized the difficulties of a barter system. It was not easy to find someone who had exactly what you wanted and was willing to exchange it for something you had. So, they came up with a brilliant idea - using certain objects as a medium of exchange. These objects had value and were easy to carry around. They could be traded for other things and acted as a common language of trade. The earliest forms of money were often commodities, such as grains, shells, and even salt. Later, as societies evolved, they began using metal objects like copper, silver, and gold as money. These metals were durable, scarce, and didn't spoil like grains. They were precious and quickly became universally accepted as a means of trade.

The Different Forms of Money

In today's world, money comes in various forms, each designed to make our lives more convenient. Let's explore the different types of money we use in our daily lives:

Coins and Bills

One of the most familiar forms of money is coins and bills. Coins are small, round pieces made from metals like copper, nickel, and zinc. They come in different denominations, representing different values, such as one cent, five cents, ten cents, and so on. Bills, on the other hand, are rectangular pieces of paper issued by the government. They are larger than coins and usually represent higher values, like one dollar, five dollars, ten dollars, and so forth. The colorful designs and pictures on coins and bills often reflect important historical figures or symbols of the country they belong to.

Digital Money

In this modern age of technology, we have another fantastic form of money—digital money. Instead of carrying physical coins and bills, we can now make transactions using our computers, smartphones, or cards. Digital money exists in the form of numbers stored in electronic databases at banks and financial institutions. When you receive your allowance or a gift from a relative, the money is often deposited into your bank account digitally. You can then use your bank card to make purchases or transfer money to others electronically. Digital money has made our lives more convenient, as we can pay for things without carrying physical cash.

Checks

Checks are another form of money that some people still use. They are like special pieces of paper that allow you to transfer money from your bank account to someone else's account. When you write a check, you are telling your bank to pay the specified amount to the person or organization named on the check. Checks were more commonly used in the past, but with the rise of digital transactions, their usage has decreased. However, they can still be helpful when paying bills or making payments to individuals who don't accept digital payments.

Prepaid Cards and Gift Cards

Prepaid cards and gift cards are a unique form of money that you can load with a specific amount of cash. They are like magic cards with a limited balance that you can use to buy things until the balance runs out.

Gift cards are often given as presents, allowing the recipient to choose what they want from a particular store. Prepaid cards, on the other hand, can be used for general purchases and are convenient for those who don't have a bank account.

Understanding the Concept of Value

Now that we know the different forms of money, let's dive deeper into the concept of "value." Have you ever wondered why certain things are more expensive than others? Why does a toy cost more than a pencil? The answer lies in their perceived value. Value is a subjective measure of how much something is worth to someone. It depends on factors like usefulness, rarity, and desirability. For example, a toy might be more valuable to you because it brings

you joy and fun, while a pencil might be more valuable to an artist who needs it for their creative work. In the world of money, we often use currency to represent the value of things. When you go to a store to buy a toy, you exchange money for the toy because the money holds value. The store believes the money is valuable because they can use it to buy other things they need for their business.

Money as an Exchange Tool

Imagine a bustling marketplace filled with colourful stalls and a variety of products. People are buying, selling, and exchanging goods. Money acts as the common language in this marketplace, allowing everyone to trade what they have for what they want. When you have money, you have the power to choose. You can use it to buy toys, books, ice cream, or save it for something special in the future. Money gives you the freedom to decide how to spend, save, or invest it to achieve your goals and dreams.

Congratulations! You've taken your first steps into the world of money - a fascinating realm where value, exchange, and dreams intertwine. In this chapter, we learned about the origins of money, explored its various forms, and understood the concept of value that drives our daily transactions.

As we continue our journey, get ready to dive deeper into the wonders of saving, investing, and financial independence. Remember, money is not just about buying things; it's a powerful tool that, when used wisely, can open doors to a world of possibilities. So, let's forge ahead to discover the secrets of making our money grow and learning how to turn our dreams into reality through investing!

Chapter 2
The Power of Saving

Imagine you have a treasure chest hidden in your room. Inside this magical chest, you can store your favourite toys, books, and even dreams. But here's the secret: this extraordinary treasure chest isn't just for collecting things; it's also a powerful tool that can help you achieve financial independence. Welcome to the wondrous world of saving - a journey that begins with the tiniest of steps but leads to mighty accomplishments.

The Importance of Saving Money

Have you ever received some money as a gift or for doing a chore around the house? It's an exciting feeling, isn't it? Now, you might be tempted to spend it all on toys, candy, or something fun right away. And that's perfectly okay - enjoying life's little pleasures is essential. However, there's a wise saying: "Don't spend all your gold in one go." And that's where the power of saving comes into play. Saving is like planting a seed. When you put some of your money aside for the future, you're sowing the seed of financial independence. The money you save doesn't vanish; it stays safe and starts to grow, just like a tiny sapling blossoms into a tall, strong tree over time. Think of saving as a way to build your future, brick by brick. With each coin you drop into your piggy bank or deposit into your savings account, you're adding a brick to the foundation of your dreams.

The Journey of a Piggy Bank

Ah, the beloved piggy bank - an iconic symbol of saving and a trusty companion on this thrilling journey. It's more than just a cute container; it's a reminder of your commitment to your financial goals. Your piggy bank stands guard, keeping your savings safe from impulse spending and encouraging you to be patient and persistent.

Let's follow the journey of your piggy bank:

Step 1: The Empty Beginning

When you first get your piggy bank, it's empty, just like a blank canvas waiting for an artist's touch. It's brimming with potential, ready to be filled with coins and bills that will grow into something amazing.

Step 2: Dropping the First Coin

The first time you drop a coin into your piggy bank, it might not feel like much. But every journey begins with a single step, and this is your first step toward financial independence.

Step 3: Slow and Steady Growth

As days turn into weeks and weeks into months, you'll watch your piggy bank grow. It might not happen quickly, but remember, great things take time. Each coin you add is like nourishment for your dream tree.

Step 4: Reaching Goals

Over time, your savings will accumulate, and you'll start reaching small goals. Maybe you'll save up for a new board game, a pair of roller skates, or even a special outing with friends.

Step 5: The Power of Patience

As you continue saving, you'll discover the power of patience. Instead of spending all your money right away, you'll learn to wait for the right moment to enjoy something truly meaningful.

Step 6: Setting Bigger Goals

With the taste of success, you'll begin setting bigger goals. Maybe you'll dream of buying a bicycle, saving for college, or even starting a small business.

Step 7: Empowering Others

Saving not only empowers you but also gives you the ability to help others. You might decide to use some of your savings to support a charity or cause you care about, spreading kindness and making a positive impact.

Step 8: Reaching the Summit

As you keep saving, you'll reach significant milestones. Your piggy bank, once empty, will now be overflowing with coins, a testament to your dedication and perseverance.

The Power of Compound Interest

Remember the magical tree of saving we mentioned earlier? Well, there's a secret ingredient that makes it grow even faster - compound interest. Compound interest is like a superpower that multiplies your money over time, helping it grow faster and stronger.

Here's how it works:

Imagine you save some money in a savings account at a bank. The bank is so impressed with your dedication to saving that they decide to reward you with a little bonus—a small amount of extra money added to your savings from time to time. Now, here's the best part: the bank doesn't just give you the bonus on your original savings; they also give it on the bonus itself!

In simple terms, compound interest allows you to earn interest on both your initial savings and the interest you've already earned. It's like a snowball rolling down a hill, picking up more snow as it goes and growing larger with each turn.

Let's look at an example:

Suppose you save $100 in a savings account with an annual interest rate of 5%. After one year, you'll have $105 in your account—the original $100 plus the $5 interest earned. But here's the magic: in the second year, you'll earn interest on $105, not just on the original $100. So, you'll earn $5.25 in interest, bringing your total savings to $110.25.

As time goes on, the interest compounds, and your savings continue to grow even if you don't add any more money. The longer you let your money grow with compound interest, the more impressive the results become!

Fun Ways to Set Savings Goals

Now that you understand the power of saving, it's time to set some exciting savings goals. Goals give you direction and purpose, making your saving journey even more thrilling. Here are some fun ways to set savings goals:

The Dream Jar

Get a clear jar or container and decorate it with your favourite colors and

stickers. This jar will be your "Dream Jar." Whenever you receive some money or decide to save, drop a coin into the jar. Before long, you'll see your Dream Jar filling up, and you can use the money to make your dreams come true!

The Three-Part Savings

Divide your money into three parts: saving, spending, and giving. When you receive money, put a portion into your piggy bank for saving, another portion for spending on things you love, and the last portion for supporting a cause or charity you care about. This way, you'll learn the importance of balancing your financial priorities.

The Savings Adventure Map

Draw a map with various savings milestones marked on it, like a treasure hunt. Each milestone represents a specific amount of money you aim to save. As you save, color in the milestones one by one, and watch your savings adventure map come to life.

The Piggy Bank Challenge

Challenge yourself to see how many coins you can add to your piggy bank each week or month. Set a goal and reward yourself with something special when you achieve it. You'll be amazed at how fast your savings grow with regular contributions.

Saving with Friends

If you have friends who also enjoy saving, why not make it a fun group activity? Create a "Saving Club" and encourage each other to save regularly. You can share your savings goals and celebrate each other's achievements. Saving together can be even more exciting and motivating!

Congratulations, young savers! You've taken the first step on your path to financial independence.

Chapter 3
The World of Investing

Welcome to a world filled with opportunities and possibilities - the world of investing! As you venture into this realm, you'll discover the secret to making your money work for you, leading you closer to the dream of financial independence. In this chapter, we'll embark on an exhilarating journey to understand what investing truly means, how it differs from saving, and explore various investment options in simple terms.

What is Investing?

If saving is like planting a seed, then investing is nurturing that seed into a flourishing garden. Investing is the process of putting your money into different assets with the expectation that it will grow over time. The goal of investing is to achieve a higher return on your money than you would with traditional saving methods, such as putting it in a piggy bank or a regular savings account.

Think of investing as a way to let your money become a little entrepreneur. Instead of just sitting in a jar or a bank, your money goes out into the world to create more money. It does this by becoming a part-owner of companies, lending money to governments and corporations, or participating in other financial opportunities.

How Investing Differs from Saving

At this point, you might be wondering, "What's the difference between saving and investing?" Let's explore their distinctions:

Purpose and Time-frame

The primary purpose of saving is to preserve and store your money for future use. It's like setting aside money for a specific goal or emergency fund, ensuring you have enough for the things you want and need. On the other hand, investing aims to make your money grow over time. It involves putting your money to work in various assets with the expectation of earning a return. Investing is more focused on long-term growth and building wealth.

Risk and Return

When you save money in a piggy bank or a savings account, it's generally safe. You don't have to worry about losing the money you saved, but the downside is that the return is relatively low. Banks pay you interest on your savings, but it might not keep up with inflation, which is the increase in prices over time.

Investing, on the other hand, carries some level of risk. Depending on the investment, the value of your money might go up or down. However, with higher risk comes the potential for higher returns. By choosing your investments wisely and diversifying your portfolio, you can manage and reduce risk while aiming for more significant gains.

Inflation and Purchasing Power

Inflation is like a sneaky monster that can erode the purchasing power of your money over time. Imagine if a toy you want costs $10 today, but due to inflation, it might cost $12 in a year. If your savings or investments don't grow at least as fast as inflation, the real value of your money decreases. While traditional saving methods like piggy banks and savings accounts might not keep pace with inflation, investing in assets that typically outperform inflation can protect and grow the purchasing power of your money.

Exploring Investment Options

Now that we have a better understanding of investing let's delve into some common investment options that you might come across:

Stocks

Stocks represent ownership in a company. When you buy a share of stock, you become a shareholder, which means you own a small part of that company. As the company grows and becomes more profitable, the value of its stock may increase, and you can sell your shares for a profit. Investing in stocks can be like riding a roller coaster. The prices can go up and down due to various factors like company performance, industry trends, and market sentiment. That's why it's essential to research companies before investing and consider a long-term perspective.

Bonds

Bonds are like lending money to the government or a company. When you buy a bond, you are essentially loaning your money to the issuer, who promises to pay you back with interest over time. Bonds are generally considered less risky than stocks because they offer more predictable returns, but the potential for high growth is limited.

Mutual Funds

Mutual funds are investment vehicles that pool money from multiple investors to buy a diversified portfolio of stocks, bonds, or other securities. By investing in a mutual fund, you get exposure to a broad range of assets, reducing the risk associated with investing in individual stocks or bonds. Mutual funds are managed by professional fund managers who make decisions about what to buy and sell based on the fund's objectives. They are an excellent option for investors who want a hands-off approach and prefer to rely on experts' expertise.

Exchange-Traded Funds (ETFs)

ETFs are similar to mutual funds in that they provide a diversified portfolio of assets. However, unlike mutual funds, ETFs trade on stock exchanges like individual stocks. This means their prices can fluctuate throughout the trading day, providing more flexibility for investors who want to buy or sell at specific times. ETFs are popular among investors due to their low expense ratios and tax efficiency. They are an accessible option for those who want to invest in various assets without the minimum investment requirements of some mutual funds.

Real Estate

Investing in real estate means buying properties like houses, apartments, or commercial buildings with the intention of generating rental income or selling them for a profit. Real estate can be a tangible and valuable asset, and its value can appreciate over time. While real estate can offer excellent returns, it requires careful research and management. Buying and maintaining properties involve costs and responsibilities, making it a more hands-on investment compared to stocks or bonds.

Inspiring Stories of Young Investors

You might be thinking, "Investing sounds fascinating, but can kids really do it?" The answer is a resounding yes! Investing knows no age limits, and there are inspiring stories of young investors who have achieved remarkable success.

Take the story of Isabella, a 12-year-old who started a small business selling handmade jewellery. With her earnings, she decided to invest a portion of her profits in the stock market. Isabella researched companies she believed in and

bought shares of their stock. Over time, her investments grew, and she learned valuable lessons about patience, research, and the power of compounding.

Then there's Alex, a 10-year-old with a passion for technology. Alex asked his parents to invest some of his birthday money in a technology-focused mutual fund. As the tech industry boomed, so did Alex's investment. He watched as his money multiplied, inspiring him to learn more about the companies he was investing in and the technology sector as a whole.

These stories show that investing isn't just for grown-ups in suits; it's for anyone with the curiosity and determination to make their money grow. With the right guidance, research, and a long-term perspective, kids like you can become successful investors and start building a bright financial future.

Congratulations on taking your first steps into the exciting world of investing! In this chapter, you learned what investing means and how it differs from saving. You explored various investment options, from stocks and bonds to mutual funds and real estate, gaining insights into their potential risks and rewards. Moreover, you discovered that investing isn't an exclusive club for adults - it's a realm where age knows no boundaries, and kids like you can achieve great success.

Chapter 4
The Marvels of Compound Interest

$10
$20
$30

Welcome to the enchanting world of compound interest - the magical force that can turn even small investments into substantial fortunes over time. In this chapter, we will unveil the wonders of compound interest, explore its incredible potential, and understand why starting early is the key to harnessing its full power.

Introducing Compound Interest

Imagine a seed planted in fertile soil. As it grows, it produces new seeds, which, in turn, grow into more plants. This cycle repeats, and before long, you have a lush and thriving garden. Compound interest works in a similar way, but instead of seeds, we have money, and instead of plants, we have wealth. At its core, compound interest is the interest earned on both the initial principal and any previously earned interest. It's like a snowball rolling down a hill, gathering more snow as it goes and growing larger and faster with each turn. The longer the snowball rolls, the more snow it accumulates, just as the longer your investments grow, the more wealth they accumulate.

The Power of Consistent Growth

The true marvel of compound interest lies in its ability to generate exponential growth. When your investments earn interest and continue to be reinvested, they grow at an accelerating rate. This consistent growth has the potential to transform even modest savings into substantial wealth over time.

To illustrate the power of compound interest, let's consider two imaginary young investors, Alex and Emma. Alex starts investing $100 each month from the age of 20 until 30, a total of $12,000. Emma, on the other hand, starts investing the same amount of $100 each month from the age of 30 until 60, a total of $36,000. Assuming both Alex and Emma earn an average annual return of 8%, let's see how their investments grow over time:

Age 30 - Alex: $12,000 (Total investment)

Age 60 - Alex: $467,048.45 (Value of investment)

Age 60 - Emma: $447,243.05 (Value of investment)

Despite investing three times more money than Alex, Emma's investments didn't surpass Alex's. This exemplifies the extraordinary advantage of starting

early. Alex had more time for his investments to benefit from compound interest, which ultimately led to a higher total value.

The Rule of 72

To estimate how long it takes for an investment to double in value with compound interest, you can use the "Rule of 72." This simple rule states that to approximate the number of years required to double your investment at a given interest rate, divide 72 by the interest rate.

For example, if your investment is expected to earn an average annual return of 8%, it would take approximately 9 years (72 ÷ 8) for your investment to double in value.

The Rule of 72 emphasizes the importance of both time and interest rate in growing your investments. The higher the interest rate and the longer your investment remains untouched, the faster your money multiplies.

The Magical Effect of Starting Early

The most potent weapon in the arsenal of compound interest is time. When you start investing early, you give your money more time to grow, and this can lead to astonishing results. Even small contributions made consistently over a long period can accumulate to substantial sums.

To highlight this magical effect, let's consider three imaginary friends: Sarah, Mike, and Chris. Each of them starts investing $50 every month at different ages. Sarah starts at age 25, Mike at age 35, and Chris at age 45. Assuming all three earn the same average annual return of 7%, let's compare their investments at age 65:

Sarah (Started at age 25): $284,136.62

Mike (Started at age 35): $138,498.88

Chris (Started at age 45): $60,570.43

Despite Sarah, Mike, and Chris contributing the same amount of money over time, Sarah's investments grew substantially more due to the advantage of starting early. The power of compound interest can be truly magical when time

is on your side.

The Perils of Delaying Investment

While starting early unleashes the full potential of compound interest, delaying investment can significantly diminish its magic. Procrastination can be costly when it comes to building wealth. Let's consider a real-world example to illustrate the perils of delaying investment:

Emma and Ben are friends who both wish to retire with $1 million. Emma starts investing $500 per month at age 25, while Ben decides to delay investing until age 35, after which he invests $1,000 per month. Assuming they both earn an average annual return of 6%, let's see how their retirement savings compare at age 65:

Emma (Started at age 25): $1,047,655.92

Ben (Started at age 35): $738,025.54

Despite investing twice the amount each month, Ben's delayed start significantly impacted his final retirement savings. Emma's investments benefited from a full decade of compound interest, giving her a substantial advantage.

The Value of Patience and Discipline

While the magic of compound interest can inspire awe, it is essential to remember that it is not an overnight miracle. Building wealth through compound interest requires patience, discipline, and a long-term perspective. Consistent contributions, even in small amounts, over an extended period will lead to remarkable results. The journey of investing and compounding wealth may face ups and downs, but staying committed to your financial goals and not being swayed by short-term fluctuations is the key to success. Embrace a disciplined approach to investing and let compound interest work its magic over time.

Diversification: A Shield Against Volatility

As you explore the wonders of compound interest, it's crucial to understand that all investments carry some level of risk. Market fluctuations can impact the

value of your investments, and the road to wealth may not always be smooth.

Diversification is a powerful shield against the volatility of the financial markets. By spreading your investments across different asset classes, such as stocks, bonds, real estate, and others, you can reduce the overall risk of your portfolio. This balanced approach helps protect your investments and ensures that the magic of compound interest continues to work for you, even during challenging times.

The Timeless Wisdom of Compound Interest

The principle of compound interest has been a guiding force for centuries, leading individuals and nations to prosperity. From ancient civilizations to modern economies, the concept of compounding has shaped financial decisions and created lasting wealth. As a young investor, you stand at the cusp of a remarkable journey - one that can transform your financial future through the marvels of compound interest. By understanding the power of starting early, remaining patient and disciplined, and embracing a diversified approach, you hold the key to unlock the magic of compound interest and set yourself on a path to financial independence.

Remember, the journey of wealth-building is not just about the destination; it's about the incredible growth and transformation that occurs along the way. Embrace the timeless wisdom of compound interest, and may its magic guide you to a future of prosperity, abundance, and fulfilment. Happy investing, and may your wealth multiply as you continue your journey of financial empowerment.

Chapter 5
Risk and Rewards

R
I
S
K

In the world of investing, the concept of risk and rewards forms the cornerstone of decision-making. As young investors, it is essential to understand the delicate balance between the potential for gains and the possibility of losses. In this chapter, we will delve into the dynamics of risk and rewards, explore how to assess risk, make informed investment decisions, and emphasize the importance of diversification and long-term thinking.

The Nature of Risk

Risk is an inherent part of investing. Every investment carries some level of uncertainty, and the value of investments can fluctuate due to various factors, including economic conditions, market sentiment, and company performance. Understanding risk is crucial as it helps you evaluate the potential challenges and rewards associated with different investment opportunities. It's important to recognize that risk does not equate to a guaranteed loss. In fact, risk and rewards are interconnected - the higher the potential for gains, the higher the level of risk. Similarly, investments with lower risk tend to offer more modest returns.

Assessing Risk Tolerance

Before diving into the world of investing, it's essential to assess your risk tolerance - the level of comfort you have with taking on risk. Risk tolerance varies from person to person and can be influenced by factors such as age, financial goals, investment experience, and emotional temperament. Some young investors may have a higher risk tolerance, as they have more time to recover from potential losses and can afford to take on greater risk in pursuit of higher rewards. Others may have a lower risk tolerance, preferring to prioritize the preservation of their capital and seeking more conservative investment options.

Diversification: Spreading the Risk

One of the most effective strategies to manage risk is diversification. Diversification involves spreading your investments across a range of different assets, industries, and geographic regions. By doing so, you reduce the impact of a significant loss in any one investment, as losses in some assets may be offset by gains in others. Imagine you have all your investment capital in a single stock of a technology company. If that company faces unexpected challenges, the value of your entire investment could plummet. However, if you

diversify your portfolio to include stocks from various industries, bonds, real estate, and other assets, the impact of a single investment's poor performance is mitigated.

The Rewards of Higher Risk

While higher risk investments can be unsettling, they also offer the potential for greater rewards. Investments like stocks and equity-based mutual funds tend to be riskier, but historically, they have provided higher average returns over the long term compared to more conservative options like bonds or cash equivalents. The key to balancing risk and rewards is to tailor your investment strategy to align with your risk tolerance, financial goals, and investment time horizon. Young investors often have the advantage of a longer investment horizon, giving them the flexibility to include higher-risk assets in their portfolios.

Long-Term Thinking: The Path to Wealth

When it comes to investing, adopting a long-term perspective is a powerful tool. While short-term market fluctuations can cause volatility, focusing on the long game allows you to weather temporary storms and stay committed to your financial goals. History has shown that the stock market, for example, experiences short-term ups and downs, but over extended periods, it has consistently trended upward. By staying invested and resisting the urge to make frequent changes based on short-term market movements, you give your investments the opportunity to grow and benefit from the power of compounding.

Avoiding Emotional Decision-Making

The world of investing is not immune to emotional influences. Fear and greed can lead investors to make impulsive decisions, such as panic selling during market downturns or chasing after the latest investment fad. Emotions can cloud judgment and lead to suboptimal outcomes. To avoid emotional decision-making, focus on your long-term financial goals, and base your investment decisions on careful research and analysis. Consider seeking guidance from financial advisors who can provide objective advice and help you stay on track with your financial plan.

Making Informed Investment Decisions

Informed decision-making is essential when navigating the landscape of risk and rewards. Here are some key factors to consider when evaluating potential investments:

Investment Objectives: Clearly define your investment objectives, whether they are long-term wealth accumulation, funding education, or buying a home. Align your investment choices with your specific goals.

Investment Horizon: Consider your investment time horizon - the period over which you plan to hold the investment. Longer horizons may allow for more exposure to higher-risk assets.

Asset Allocation: Create a well-balanced asset allocation strategy that reflects your risk tolerance and diversifies your investments across various asset classes.

Research and Analysis: Conduct thorough research on the investments you are considering. Evaluate the financial health of companies, study market trends, and understand the economic factors that may impact your investments.

Risk Management: Implement risk management strategies, such as stop-loss orders for individual stocks or using hedging techniques for a portfolio, to limit potential losses.

Regular Review: Periodically review your investment portfolio and make adjustments as needed to keep it in line with your changing goals and risk tolerance.

Learning from Mistakes

Investing is a continuous learning process, and it's normal to make mistakes along the way. If an investment does not perform as expected, use it as an opportunity to reflect, learn, and adjust your approach. Successful investors understand that learning from failures is a stepping stone to success.

Embracing a Balanced Approach

As you navigate the interplay of risk and rewards, remember that no single investment strategy fits all. The key is to find a balanced approach that aligns

with your financial goals and risk tolerance. While higher-risk assets offer the potential for greater rewards, they also come with increased uncertainty. Conservative investments, on the other hand, may provide stability but with more modest returns. A diversified portfolio, tailored to your unique circumstances, can help you strike a balance between risk and rewards. By staying disciplined, embracing long-term thinking, and making informed decisions, you can confidently navigate the world of investing and move closer to achieving your financial goals.

Embracing the Journey

As young investors, you are embarking on a transformative journey - one that embraces both the excitement of potential rewards and the cautiousness of managing risks. The world of investing is full of opportunities and challenges, and it is your courage and resilience that will guide you through this thrilling adventure.

Remember that risk and rewards are intertwined, and the path to wealth is a dynamic one. Embrace diversification to protect your investments, adopt a long-term perspective to capitalize on the power of compounding, and remain focused on your financial goals. As you navigate this chapter of your financial education, may you develop the wisdom to recognize opportunities, the fortitude to withstand uncertainties, and the patience to see your investments grow over time. May your journey be filled with valuable experiences, valuable lessons, and the fulfilment of your aspirations. Happy investing, and may the delicate dance of risk and rewards lead you toward a prosperous and rewarding future.

Chapter 6
Setting Financial Goals

In the quest for financial independence, setting clear and achievable goals is the compass that guides your journey. As young investors, defining your financial goals lays the foundation for a purposeful and successful investment strategy. In this chapter, we will explore the significance of setting financial goals, understand the different types of goals, and learn how to create a simple plan that incorporates both saving and investing strategies.

The Power of Setting Goals

Imagine embarking on a journey without a destination in mind. Without a clear sense of where you want to go, you may find yourself wandering aimlessly, unsure of the path to take. Setting financial goals gives your journey a purpose - a target to aim for and a roadmap to follow. Financial goals provide direction and motivation. They serve as milestones to measure your progress and celebrate your achievements. Whether it's saving for a dream vacation, funding your education, buying a home, or achieving early retirement, setting goals empowers you to take charge of your financial future.

Types of Financial Goals

Financial goals can be broadly categorized into three main types:

Short-Term Goals: Short-term goals typically have a timeline of one year or less. These goals often involve funding immediate expenses or achieving specific milestones. Examples include saving for a new smartphone, funding a weekend getaway, or purchasing a new gaming console.

Medium-Term Goals: Medium-term goals have a timeline of one to five years. These goals often require more significant financial planning and may involve saving for a down payment on a car, funding a college education, or planning for a wedding.

Long-Term Goals: Long-term goals extend beyond five years and often revolve around major life events or financial milestones. Examples include saving for retirement, purchasing a home, or building a substantial investment portfolio.

Defining Your Financial Goals

To set meaningful financial goals, it's essential to take a thoughtful and introspective approach. Here are some steps to help you define your goals:

Reflect on Your Aspirations: Consider what you want to achieve in the short, medium, and long term. Identify your dreams, desires, and priorities.

Prioritize Your Goals: Rank your goals based on their importance and urgency. Focus on one or two primary goals at a time, as spreading your resources too thin may hinder progress.

Be Specific and Measurable: Set clear, specific, and measurable goals. Instead of saying, "I want to save more money," specify the amount you want to save and by when.

Make Goals Realistic: While it's important to dream big, ensure your goals are achievable given your current financial situation and resources.

Set a Timeline: Assign a timeline to each goal. This creates a sense of urgency and helps you track your progress.

Write Them Down: Putting your goals in writing solidifies your commitment to them. Use a journal, digital document, or goal-setting app to record your financial aspirations.

Creating a Simple Financial Plan

Once you have defined your financial goals, it's time to create a simple financial plan that aligns with your objectives. Here's how you can go about it:

Assess Your Current Financial Situation: Review your income, expenses, assets, and debts. Understanding your financial standing provides a starting point for your plan.

Budgeting: Create a budget that allocates your income towards essential expenses, savings, and investments. A budget helps you manage your money effectively and ensures you're on track to meet your goals.

Emergency Fund: Before diving into long-term investments, establish an emergency fund. This fund, equivalent to three to six months' worth of living expenses, acts as a safety net during unexpected financial challenges.

Short-Term Goals: Prioritize funding your short-term goals. Allocate a portion of your savings towards achieving these goals within their designated timeline.

Medium and Long-Term Goals: Once your short-term goals are covered, shift your focus to medium and long-term goals. Determine the amount you need to save or invest to achieve these objectives.

Investment Strategies: Choose investment vehicles that align with your goals and risk tolerance. Consider a mix of stocks, bonds, mutual funds, and other investment options to diversify your portfolio.

Regular Review: Periodically review your financial plan and adjust it as needed. Life circumstances change, and your plan should adapt accordingly.

The Importance of Saving

Saving is the bedrock of achieving your financial goals. It provides the capital needed for investments and acts as a buffer during times of financial uncertainty. Cultivating good saving habits at a young age sets the stage for a financially secure future. Automating your savings is an effective way to ensure consistent contributions. Consider setting up automatic transfers from your checking account to a savings or investment account. This way, you'll prioritize saving before spending, making it easier to stay on track with your goals.

The Art of Delayed Gratification

As young investors, you may face temptations to spend your money on immediate desires rather than saving for the future. However, mastering the art of delayed gratification is a powerful skill that can set you apart in your financial journey. Delayed gratification involves resisting the impulse to spend now in favour of achieving more significant rewards in the future. It allows you to prioritize your long-term goals and build a foundation of discipline and self-control. One way to practice delayed gratification is to set up a "reward" system for reaching milestones in your financial plan. Treat yourself to something special or celebrate your achievements once you've reached a particular savings or investment target. This positive reinforcement can motivate you to stay on course with your financial goals.

Building a Financial Safety Net

As you strive to achieve your financial goals, it's essential to build a financial safety net to protect against unexpected setbacks. This safety net includes an emergency fund and insurance coverage.

An emergency fund, as mentioned earlier, provides a cushion during times of financial hardship. It prevents you from dipping into your long-term investments or incurring high-interest debt to cover unexpected expenses.

Insurance, such as health insurance, auto insurance, and renters or homeowners insurance, safeguards you from significant financial losses due to accidents, illnesses, or property damage. By having a robust financial safety net, you create a buffer that allows you to continue pursuing your long-term goals without being derailed by unforeseen circumstances.

Embracing Flexibility and Adaptability

As you embark on your financial journey and work towards your goals, remember that life is dynamic, and circumstances may change. Embrace flexibility and adaptability in your financial plan. If your goals evolve or you encounter unexpected opportunities, be open to adjusting your strategy.

Tracking Your Progress

Tracking your progress towards your financial goals is vital to staying motivated and making necessary adjustments. Here are some tips for effective goal tracking:

Regular Check-ins: Set aside time every month or quarter to review your financial progress. Assess how close you are to reaching your goals and whether any changes are needed.

Record Keeping: Keep a record of your savings, investments, and expenses. Use spreadsheets, financial apps, or journals to monitor your financial activity.

Celebrate Milestones: Celebrate each milestone you achieve along the way. Acknowledging your progress boosts your confidence and reinforces positive financial habits.

Reassess and Adjust: If you encounter challenges or unexpected changes, reassess your goals and make adjustments as necessary. Financial planning is not rigid; it should adapt to your life circumstances.

The Journey of Financial Growth

As you embark on the path of setting financial goals, remember that it is a

journey of growth and learning. The goals you set today may evolve as you progress through different life stages and gain new experiences. Embrace this evolution and recognize that it's a natural part of the financial journey.

Setting financial goals empowers you with purpose, direction, and control over your financial future. It enables you to allocate your resources wisely and prioritize your dreams. As you pursue your goals with diligence, patience, and determination, may you unlock the door to financial independence and pave the way to a life of abundance and fulfilment. Happy goal-setting, and may each milestone bring you closer to your aspirations!

Chapter 7
Starting Your Investment Journey

Congratulations on embarking on your investment journey - a path filled with endless possibilities and opportunities for financial growth. In this chapter, we'll take practical steps to help you kickstart your investment journey, from opening an investment account to researching potential investments and tracking progress toward your financial goals. By equipping you with the right knowledge and tools, you'll be well-prepared to navigate the exciting world of investing.

Building the Foundation: Assess Your Financial Situation

Before diving into the world of investing, it's essential to build a strong foundation by assessing your financial situation. Understanding your current financial standing will help you set realistic goals and make informed investment decisions.

Here are some steps to assess your financial situation:

Calculate Your Net Worth: Determine your net worth by subtracting your total liabilities (debts) from your total assets (savings, investments, possessions, etc.). This calculation provides an overview of your financial health.

Evaluate Your Income and Expenses: Analyse your income sources and expenses to understand your cash flow. Knowing how much money you have available for investing after covering essential expenses will guide your investment strategy.

Define Your Financial Goals: Revisit the financial goals you set in Chapter 6 and ensure they align with your current financial situation. Consider any adjustments based on your assessment.

Opening an Investment Account

To begin investing, you'll need an investment account—a place to buy, sell, and hold your investments. There are various types of investment accounts, each with its advantages and considerations:

Custodial Accounts: If you're a minor, a custodial account allows a parent or guardian to manage investments on your behalf until you reach the legal age of adulthood.

Individual Retirement Accounts (IRAs): IRAs are tax-advantaged accounts designed for long-term retirement savings. There are traditional IRAs, where contributions may be tax-deductible, and Roth IRAs, where withdrawals in retirement are tax-free.

401(k) or 403(b) Accounts: These are employer-sponsored retirement accounts, often with employer matching contributions. If your parent or guardian has a 401(k) or 403(b) account through their employer, they may be able to open a custodial account for you.

Brokerage Accounts: A brokerage account allows you to invest in a wide range of assets, including stocks, bonds, mutual funds, ETFs, and more. Some brokerage accounts have no minimum balance requirements, making them accessible to young investors.

Robo-Advisor Accounts: Robo-advisors are automated investment platforms that use algorithms to build and manage portfolios based on your risk tolerance and financial goals. They are user-friendly and often require lower minimum investments.

When opening an investment account, ensure that you consider factors such as fees, account minimums, investment options, and customer support.

Researching Potential Investments

As an aspiring investor, research is your superpower - the tool that helps you make informed decisions and choose investments that align with your goals and risk tolerance. Here are some essential steps to conduct thorough research:

Understand Different Investment Options: Familiarize yourself with various investment options, such as stocks, bonds, mutual funds, ETFs, real estate, and others. Learn about their characteristics, potential risks, and historical performance.

Evaluate Investment Risks: Assess the risks associated with each investment option. Consider factors such as market risk, business risk, credit risk, inflation risk, and liquidity risk.

Analyse Historical Performance: Look at the historical performance of investments over different time periods. While past performance doesn't

guarantee future results, it can provide valuable insights.

Diversify Your Portfolio: Diversification is a crucial strategy to reduce risk. Aim to build a portfolio with a mix of assets to spread risk and potentially increase returns.

Consider Professional Advice: If you're unsure about how to conduct research or make investment decisions, seek guidance from a financial advisor. An advisor can help create a personalized investment plan based on your goals and risk tolerance.

Investing Wisely: Tips for Young Investors

As a young investor, adopting smart investing practices will set you on a path to success. Here are some tips to help you invest wisely:

Start Small: Begin with a conservative investment approach, especially if you're new to investing. Invest smaller amounts and gradually increase as you gain confidence and experience.

Focus on Long-Term: Investing is a journey that rewards patience and long-term thinking. Avoid making impulsive decisions based on short-term market fluctuations.

Keep Emotions in Check: Investing can evoke emotions like fear and greed. Stay disciplined and avoid making investment decisions based on emotions.

Set Clear Goals: Align your investment strategy with your financial goals. Each investment should have a purpose within your overall financial plan.

Avoid Chasing Hot Stocks: It's easy to be swayed by stories of "hot" stocks or investments. Focus on the fundamentals and avoid chasing short-lived trends.

Tracking Progress and Making Adjustments

As you set your investment journey in motion, it's crucial to monitor your progress regularly. Tracking your investments will help you stay on course and make any necessary adjustments to your strategy. Here are some steps to keep track of your investments:

Review Your Portfolio: Periodically review your investment portfolio to assess its performance and how it aligns with your goals. Make adjustments if your portfolio has drifted away from your target allocation.

Rebalance Your Portfolio: Over time, certain investments in your portfolio may perform better or worse than others, altering your original asset allocation. Rebalancing involves adjusting your investments to bring them back to their intended proportions.

Stay Informed: Keep yourself updated on financial news and economic trends that may impact your investments. Stay informed but avoid making knee-jerk reactions based on headlines.

Evaluate Your Goals: As your life evolves, your financial goals may change. Reassess your goals periodically to ensure they remain relevant and achievable.

Embracing the Investment Journey

Embarking on an investment journey is like setting sail on a grand adventure. It requires courage, curiosity, and a willingness to learn. Embrace the process with an open mind, knowing that every step, whether smooth or challenging, contributes to your growth as an investor. Remember that investing is a continuous learning experience. Be patient with yourself, celebrate your achievements, and learn from any setbacks. The journey of a young investor is filled with exciting possibilities, and with determination and perseverance, you'll navigate the financial waters with confidence and achieve your dreams of financial independence.

As you set sail on your investment journey, let curiosity be your compass, knowledge be your anchor, and passion be your guiding star. May your investment voyage lead you to a treasure trove of financial success and a bright future ahead. Happy investing!

Chapter 8
Protecting Your Finances: Understanding Insurance

INSURANCE
POLICY

As young investors, you have learned the art of saving and investing to grow your wealth. But what happens when life throws unexpected challenges your way? In the pursuit of financial independence, safeguarding your hard-earned money and investments is of paramount importance. One of the most effective tools for protecting your finances is insurance. Insurance serves as a safety net that shields you from the financial repercussions of unexpected events and provides peace of mind in times of uncertainty. In this chapter, we will delve into the world of insurance, understand its different types, explore how insurance works, and learn how to make informed decisions to safeguard your financial well-being.

The Significance of Insurance

Life is full of uncertainties, and unforeseen events can disrupt even the most carefully laid financial plans. Whether it's a medical emergency, a car accident, a natural disaster, or an unexpected liability claim, the financial consequences can be devastating. Insurance is designed to protect you from such risks and prevent you from facing crippling financial losses. At its core, insurance is a contract between you and an insurance company. In exchange for paying premiums, the insurance company agrees to provide financial compensation in the event of covered losses or damages. This compensation helps you recover from the financial impact of unfortunate events, allowing you to rebuild and move forward.

Types of Insurance

The insurance market offers a wide range of coverage options to address different aspects of life's uncertainties. Here are some common types of insurance you may encounter:

Health Insurance: Health insurance covers medical expenses, including hospitalization, doctor visits, prescription medications, and preventive care. Having health insurance ensures that you can access quality healthcare without facing exorbitant out-of-pocket costs.

Auto Insurance: Auto insurance protects you against financial losses arising from car accidents, theft, or damage to your vehicle. It also provides liability coverage if you are responsible for causing injuries or property damage to others.

Homeowners/Renters Insurance: Homeowners insurance covers your home and its contents against damage or loss due to events like fire, theft, vandalism, and natural disasters. Renters insurance offers similar coverage for tenants, protecting their personal belongings and providing liability coverage.

Life Insurance: Life insurance provides a payout to your beneficiaries upon your death. It is designed to provide financial support to your loved ones and cover expenses such as funeral costs, mortgage payments, and college tuition.

Disability Insurance: Disability insurance replaces a portion of your income if you become disabled and are unable to work. This coverage helps you maintain your financial stability and meet living expenses during periods of disability.

Long-Term Care Insurance: Long-term care insurance covers the costs of nursing home care, assisted living facilities, and in-home care services for individuals who need ongoing assistance with daily living activities due to ageing or a disability.

Umbrella Insurance: Umbrella insurance provides additional liability coverage that extends beyond the limits of your home and auto insurance policies. It offers protection against large liability claims that could threaten your assets and financial well-being.

How Insurance Works

Understanding how insurance works is essential to ensure you choose the right coverage and receive the support you need in times of need. Here's a simplified breakdown of how insurance functions:

Premiums: Insurance coverage requires you to pay premiums, which are regular payments to the insurance company. The premium amount depends on the type of coverage, the level of protection, your risk profile, and other factors.

Insured and Insurer: You, as the policyholder, are the insured party. The insurance company that provides coverage is the insurer.

Policy: The insurance contract is known as the policy. It outlines the terms and conditions of the coverage, including the events or risks covered, the exclusions, the premium amount, and the duration of coverage.

Coverage Limit: The policy specifies the maximum amount the insurer will pay for covered losses. This limit varies depending on the type of insurance and the policy you select.

Deductible: The deductible is the amount you must pay out of pocket before the insurance coverage kicks in. For example, if you have a $500 deductible on your auto insurance and incur $2,000 in damages, you would pay the first $500, and the insurance company would cover the remaining $1,500.

Claims Process: In the event of a covered loss, you file a claim with the insurance company. The insurer assesses the claim and, if approved, provides the compensation as per the terms of the policy.

Policy Renewal: Insurance policies have a specific duration, typically one year. At the end of the policy term, you have the option to renew the coverage by paying the renewal premium.

Evaluating Your Insurance Needs

Choosing the right insurance coverage requires a thoughtful evaluation of your financial circumstances, lifestyle, and risk exposure. Here are some factors to consider when assessing your insurance needs:

Personal Circumstances: Consider your age, marital status, dependents, and financial responsibilities. Life insurance, for instance, may be more crucial for individuals with dependents who rely on their income.

Health and Wellness: Evaluate your health status and potential medical needs. If you have pre-existing conditions or a family history of certain illnesses, comprehensive health insurance is essential.

Assets and Liabilities: Take stock of your assets, including your home, vehicles, savings, and investments. Ensure you have adequate coverage to protect these assets from unforeseen events.

Career and Income: Your career and income level impact your ability to recover from financial setbacks. Disability insurance can be particularly valuable if you rely heavily on your income to meet living expenses.

Risk Tolerance: Assess your risk tolerance - the level of comfort you have with

taking on financial risk. Insurance can help mitigate risks and provide peace of mind, especially for risk-averse individuals.

Regional Considerations: Consider the geographical area you live in and its exposure to specific risks, such as natural disasters or crime rates. Homeowners and renters insurance should reflect the unique risks of your region.

Future Goals: Think about your long-term goals and how insurance can protect those aspirations. For example, life insurance can help secure your family's financial future even in your absence.

Avoiding Over-Insurance and Under-Insurance

While having adequate insurance coverage is crucial, it's also essential to avoid over-insurance or under-insurance. Over-insurance means paying for coverage you don't need, which can result in unnecessary expenses. Under-insurance, on the other hand, leaves you vulnerable to significant financial losses in the event of a claim.

To strike the right balance:

Review Your Policies: Periodically review your insurance policies to ensure they align with your current needs and circumstances. Life changes, such as marriage, having children, or purchasing a new home, may necessitate adjustments to your coverage.

Seek Professional Advice: Consider consulting with an insurance advisor or financial planner. They can help you assess your insurance needs and tailor a comprehensive protection plan.

Bundle Policies: In some cases, bundling multiple insurance policies with the same insurer can lead to discounts and cost savings.

Shop Around: Compare insurance options from different companies to find the best coverage at competitive rates. Keep in mind that cost should not be the sole factor; the quality of coverage and customer service are also essential considerations.

Read and Understand Your Policy: Familiarize yourself with the terms and conditions of your insurance policies. Understand the coverage limits, exclusions, and the claims process.

The Importance of Regular Review

As your life evolves, so do your insurance needs. Regularly reviewing your insurance coverage ensures that you stay adequately protected. Here are some instances when a review is particularly essential:

Life Changes: Major life events, such as marriage, divorce, having children, or changes in employment, can impact your insurance needs. Review your coverage when such events occur.

Policy Renewals: Take the opportunity to review your coverage when your policies are up for renewal. Ensure the coverage still aligns with your needs and circumstances.

Changes in Assets: If you acquire significant assets, such as a new home or valuable personal property, adjust your coverage accordingly to protect these assets.

Changes in Health: Changes in your health status may impact your eligibility for certain types of insurance or affect premium rates.

Financial Milestones: As you achieve financial milestones, such as paying off debts or accumulating savings, review your insurance needs to ensure you maintain adequate protection.

The Benefits of Insurance Education

As a young investor, educating yourself about insurance is an invaluable investment in your financial literacy. Understanding insurance concepts, terms, and the different types of coverage empowers you to make informed decisions that protect your financial future.

Consider seeking out educational resources, workshops, or online courses that provide insights into insurance and risk management. Familiarize yourself with reputable insurance providers, customer reviews, and industry best practices to ensure you choose reliable coverage.

Making Informed Insurance Decisions

When it comes to insurance, making informed decisions is critical to securing the protection you need. Here are some tips to help you navigate the process:

Research and Compare: Research different insurance companies, coverage options, and premium rates. Compare the features and benefits of various policies to find the best fit for your needs.

Read the Fine Print: Carefully read the policy documents, including the terms and conditions, exclusions, and coverage limits. Ask questions and seek clarification if anything is unclear.

Seek Professional Advice: Consult with an insurance advisor or financial planner, especially when making significant insurance decisions or customizing coverage to suit your specific needs.

Review Regularly: As mentioned earlier, regularly review your insurance coverage to ensure it remains adequate and relevant to your life circumstances.

Maintain Good Records: Keep copies of all insurance-related documents, including policy details, premium payments, and claim records. Organized records simplify the claims process and ensure you have access to critical information when needed.

The Power of Peace of Mind

While insurance may seem like an additional expense, it provides something invaluable: peace of mind. Knowing that you and your loved ones are protected from the financial ramifications of unexpected events can alleviate stress and anxiety. Insurance allows you to focus on your financial goals and aspirations, confident that your hard-earned assets and investments are shielded from life's uncertainties. As you progress on your journey to financial independence, prioritize insurance as a key pillar of your protection and security.

In the ever-changing landscape of life, insurance stands as a steadfast shield, guarding against unforeseen storms and paving the way for a brighter, more secure future. By embracing the power of insurance and making informed

decisions, you embark on a path of financial resilience, empowering you to navigate any challenge that comes your way.

Chapter 9
The Impact of Giving

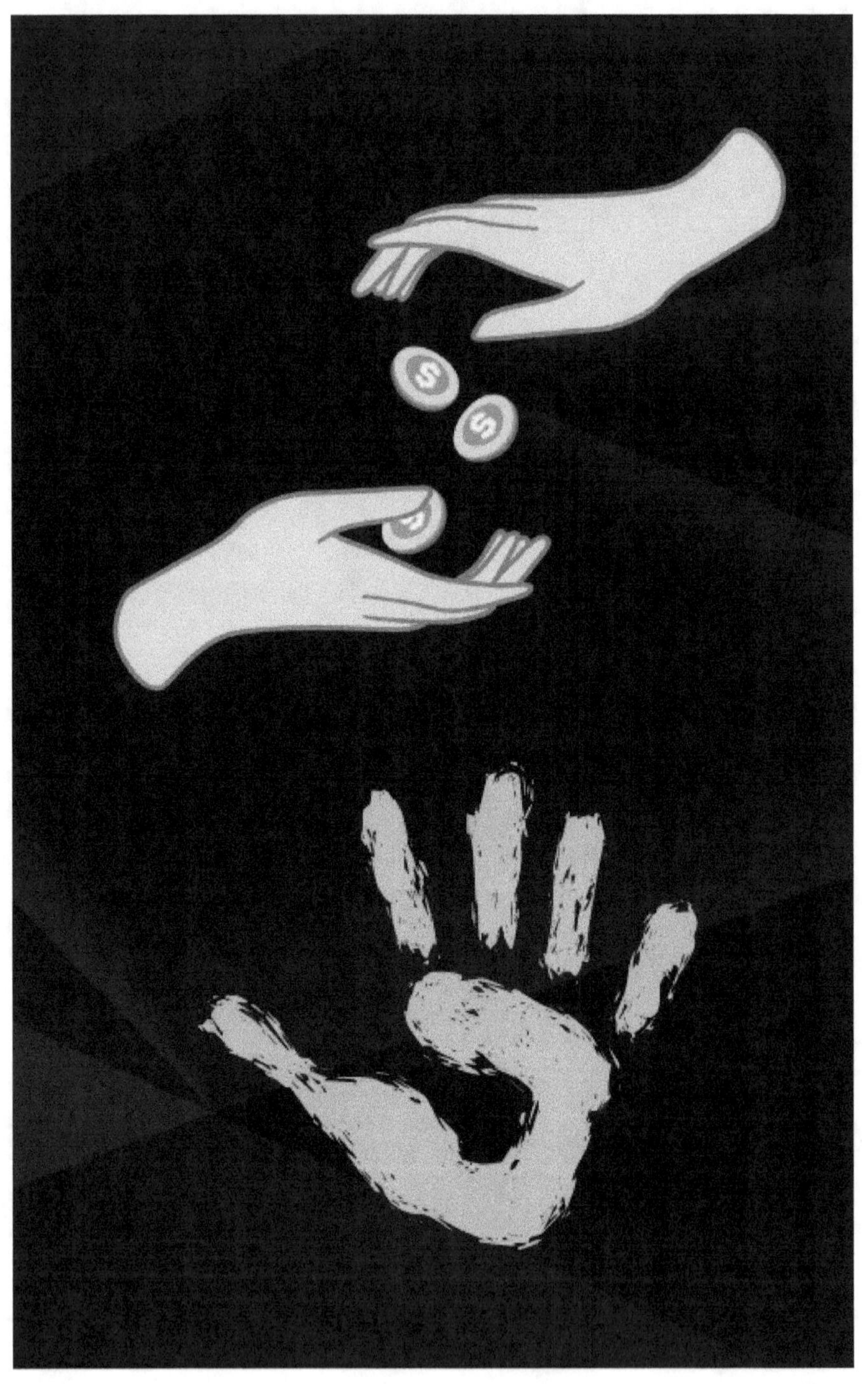

As young investors, you possess a remarkable superpower - the power to make a difference in the world. Investing isn't solely about financial gains; it can also serve as a force for positive change. In this chapter, we'll explore the concept of socially responsible investing and how you can use your investments to support causes you care about. Get ready to unleash the extraordinary potential of your investments to create a brighter and more compassionate world.

The Power of Socially Responsible Investing

Imagine a world where every investment made a positive impact - a world where your money not only grows but also supports causes that align with your values. Socially responsible investing, also known as sustainable or ethical investing, empowers you to invest in companies that demonstrate a commitment to social and environmental responsibility. With socially responsible investing, you can support businesses that champion environmental sustainability, promote social justice, prioritize employee well-being, and uphold ethical practices. By directing your investments toward these companies, you can influence corporate behaviour and encourage positive change on a global scale.

Understanding Socially Responsible Investing

Socially responsible investing encompasses various approaches to aligning your investments with your values. Let's explore some key strategies:

Screening Investments: One common approach involves screening out companies involved in controversial industries like tobacco, weapons, or fossil fuels. This negative screening ensures that your investments do not support activities that may harm society or the environment.

Positive Selection: Another approach involves actively selecting companies that excel in sustainability practices, diversity and inclusion, community engagement, and ethical governance. By investing in these companies, you promote their positive impact on society.

Impact Investing: Impact investing goes beyond merely avoiding harmful industries. It seeks to invest in companies and projects that have a measurable and intentional positive impact, such as renewable energy projects or affordable housing initiatives.

Shareholder Advocacy: As an investor, you can use your shareholder rights to advocate for positive change within companies. By engaging in shareholder activism, you can influence corporate policies and practices, encouraging greater responsibility.

How Kids Can Engage in Socially Responsible Investing

As young investors, you may wonder how you can actively engage in socially responsible investing. While you may not have complete control over your investment decisions, there are several steps you can take to align your investments with your values:

Research Companies: Learn about the companies you're interested in investing in. Look for information on their sustainability practices, ethical policies, and social initiatives. Many companies publish annual sustainability reports that highlight their efforts in these areas.

Choose Responsible Funds: If you invest through mutual funds or ETFs, look for socially responsible funds that follow sustainable investment strategies. These funds are designed to include companies with strong environmental, social, and governance (ESG) performance.

Involve Your Parents: If you're not yet of legal age to make investment decisions on your own, involve your parents or guardians in your socially responsible investing journey. Discuss your interests and values with them and explore investment options together.

Support Impactful Causes: Consider investing in companies that focus on causes you care about deeply. For example, if you're passionate about environmental conservation, seek out companies that are leaders in sustainability practices.

Promote Community Engagement: Look for companies that actively engage with their local communities and contribute positively to society. Supporting companies that prioritize community development can have a lasting impact.

The Ripple Effect of Socially Responsible Investing

Every investment you make can send ripples of change throughout the world. By supporting socially responsible companies, you contribute to a broader

movement toward sustainability, social justice, and ethical practices. Your investments become a vote of confidence, endorsing businesses that prioritize people and the planet alongside profits.

Environmental Impact: Investing in companies that prioritize environmental sustainability can help drive the transition to a greener and cleaner future. These companies may focus on reducing carbon emissions, conserving natural resources, and developing renewable energy solutions.

Social Impact: Socially responsible investing can champion social justice and equality. By investing in companies that prioritize diversity and inclusion, fair labor practices, and community development, you help create a more equitable society.

Corporate Accountability: As a socially responsible investor, you encourage corporate accountability and transparency. Companies are more likely to adopt responsible practices when they know their shareholders care about social and environmental impact.

Shaping the Future: Young investors have a unique opportunity to shape the future. Your investment choices send a powerful message to companies and investors alike, emphasizing the importance of responsible and sustainable practices.

Investing for a Better Tomorrow

As you embark on your socially responsible investing journey, remember that every dollar you invest can make a positive difference. Your investments have the potential to drive meaningful change, transform industries, and create a brighter future for generations to come.

Aligning with Your Values: Investing with purpose allows you to align your financial decisions with your values and beliefs. By investing in companies that reflect your principles, you become an agent of change in the investment landscape.

Starting Small, Making an Impact: While you may be starting with modest investments, the impact of socially responsible investing is far-reaching. Remember that even small contributions can contribute to significant changes when combined with others who share the same vision.

Building a Legacy: As a young investor, you have the potential to build a legacy of positive change. By making socially responsible investing a lifelong practice, you demonstrate the power of investing with intention and compassion.

Amplifying Your Voice: Share your passion for socially responsible investing with others. Encourage your family, friends, and community to join you in investing for a better tomorrow.

Investing in a Brighter Future

As you embrace the impact of giving through socially responsible investing, you become a steward of positive change. Your investments have the potential to create a world that values people, the environment, and the greater good.

Remember, investing is not just about accumulating wealth - it's about using that wealth to create a positive impact. Embrace your role as a young investor and harness the power of your investments to make the world a better place. Together, we can shape a future that is sustainable, just, and filled with hope for all. Happy investing, and may your journey be filled with purpose and compassion.

Conclusion

FINANCIAL
INDEPENDENCE

Congratulations, young investors, on completing your adventurous journey through the world of investing! In "Investing Money: A Fun Guide for Kids Ages 8-12 to Financial Independence," you have unlocked the secrets of money, learned the art of saving and investing, and discovered the remarkable power of your investments to create a positive impact on the world. As you stand at the end of this exciting expedition, you are now equipped with the tools and knowledge to embark on your path to financial independence.

Throughout this book, you have learned the fundamentals of money - what it is, how to save it wisely, and the wonders of investing. You've explored the magic of compound interest and the delicate balance between risk and rewards. We delved into the power of setting realistic financial goals and creating a simple plan to achieve them, combining saving and investing strategies.

You've also discovered that investing isn't just about personal gain - it's a potent force for positive change. By embracing socially responsible investing, you can direct your investments towards causes you care about deeply, shaping a world that values sustainability, equality, and ethical practices.

As young investors, your journey has just begun. The knowledge and skills you've gained will serve as a compass, guiding you through the twists and turns of the financial landscape. You have the power to make a difference not only in your own life but also in the lives of others and the well-being of our planet.

Now, as you close this chapter of learning, I invite you to take one final step - to share your thoughts and experiences with the world. I encourage you to review "Investing Money: A Fun Guide for Kids Ages 8-12 to Financial Independence" and let others know about the incredible journey that awaits them within these pages.

Your reviews and feedback are invaluable to me as they help me understand how this book has impacted your understanding of money, saving, and investing. Your words can inspire other young minds to embark on their investment journeys and embrace the wonders of financial independence. So, I kindly request you to take a moment to leave your review on your favourite bookselling platform or share your thoughts with your friends and family.

I hope this book has ignited a passion for investing within you - one that will continue to grow as you navigate the exciting world of finance. Remember, investing is not just about accumulating wealth; it's about using that wealth to

create a positive impact on the world. Your journey to financial independence is a grand adventure, and we can't wait to see how you shape a brighter future for yourself and others.

Thank you for joining me on this exhilarating ride, and I look forward to hearing about the remarkable impact your investments will make in the years to come. Happy investing, young adventurers, and may your financial journey be filled with prosperity, compassion, and joy!

With warmest regards,

Simi Subhramanian